Audit Report

Report Number: OIG-SBLF-14-010

STATE SMALL BUSINESS CREDIT INITIATIVE:
Idaho's Use of Federal Funds for its Collateral Support Program

May 19, 2014

Office of Inspector General

Department of the Treasury

Contents

Results in Brief 3
Background 4
    Idaho's Participation in SSBCI 5
Idaho Used Funds Appropriately, But Financed Loans that May Cause Duplicate Reporting of Benefits from SBA CDC/504 Loan Program 6
Idaho Did Not Accurately Report Amount of Loans Supported by SSBCI Funds 8
Idaho Reported Subsequent Private Financing Without Explicit Approval from Treasury 9
Idaho's Administrative Expenses Were Allowable, Allocable, and Reasonable 10
Recommendations 10
Management Comments and OIG Response 11
Appendix 1: Objective, Scope, and Methodology 12
Appendix 2: Management Response 14
Appendix 3: Major Contributors 18
Appendix 4: Distribution List 19

Abbreviations

ICSP	Idaho Collateral Support Program
IHFA	Idaho Housing and Finance Association
OIG	Office of Inspector General
OMB	Office of Management and Budget
SBA	Small Business Administration
SSBCI	State Small Business Credit Initiative
The Act	Small Business Jobs Act of 2010

OIG

Audit Report

The Department of the Treasury
Office of Inspector General

May 19, 2014

Mr. Amias Gerety
Acting Assistant Secretary for Financial Institutions

This report presents the results of our audit of the state of Idaho's use of funds awarded under the State Small Business Credit Initiative (SSBCI), which was established by the Small Business Jobs Act of 2010 (the Act). In August 2011, the Department of the Treasury (Treasury) awarded Idaho approximately $13.2 million,[1] which Idaho allocated in its entirety to the Idaho Collateral Support Program (ICSP). In May 2013, Treasury reduced Idaho's allocation to approximately $13.1 million[2] to exclude inadequately supported administrative expenses. As of September 30, 2013, the State had received all of its $13.1 million in allocated funds, and had obligated or spent approximately $12.7 million[3] on loans enrolled in ICSP.

The Act requires the Treasury Office of Inspector General (OIG) to conduct audits of the use of funds made available under SSBCI and to identify any instances of reckless or intentional misuse. Treasury has defined reckless misuse as a use of funds that the participating state or administering entity should have known was unauthorized or prohibited, and which is a highly unreasonable departure or willful disregard from the standards of ordinary care. Intentional misuse is any unauthorized or prohibited use of funds that the participating state or its administering entity knew was unauthorized or prohibited. Our

---

[1] Rounded up from $13,168,350.
[2] Rounded down from $13,136,544.
[3] Rounded up from $12,655,537.

Idaho's Use of Federal Funds for its Collateral Support Program

audit objective was to test participant compliance with program requirements and prohibitions to identify any reckless or intentional misuse of funds. To test participant compliance, we reviewed a statistical sample of 30 business loans enrolled in ICSP, totaling $50.3 million,[4] for which Idaho provided $7.6 million[5] in collateral. We also reviewed 12 loans that were committed for enrollment into ICSP, totaling $10.8 million,[6] as of September 30, 2013, for which Idaho had reserved $2 million[7] in collateral. We reviewed the loans to determine whether they complied with program requirements for use of proceeds, capital at risk, and other restrictions in the Act, *SSBCI Policy Guidelines*, *SSBCI National Standards for Compliance and Oversight*, and other Treasury guidance.

We also sent written inquiries to management and staff from the Idaho Department of Commerce and its contractor, the Idaho Housing and Finance Association (IHFA), which administers and reports on SSBCI funding. Additionally, we reviewed administrative costs charged against SSBCI funds to ensure they were reasonable, allowable, and allocable in accordance with *SSBCI Policy Guidelines* and Office of Management and Budget (OMB) Circular A-87, *Cost Principles for State, Local, and Indian Tribal Governments*.[8] Appendix 1 contains a more detailed description of our audit objective, scope, and methodology.

We conducted our audit from December 2013 to March 2014 in accordance with *Government Auditing Standards*. Those standards require that we plan and perform the audit to obtain sufficient, appropriate evidence to provide a reasonable basis for our findings and conclusions based on our audit objective. We believe that the evidence obtained to address our audit objective provides a reasonable basis for our findings and conclusions.

---

[4] Rounded down from $50,330,306.
[5] Rounded up from $7,577,407.
[6] Rounded down from $10,814,704.
[7] Rounded up from $1,985,490.
[8] Revised May 10, 2004.

Results in Brief

We determined that Idaho appropriately used the $9.6 million[9] in SSBCI funds that we tested. However, $1.3 million[10] financed bridge loans to businesses approved for Small Business Administration (SBA) CDC/504 loan program. Because the SSBCI-supported loans provided interim financing until the SBA loans could be secured, the transactions were permissible under *SSBCI Policy Guidelines*. However, Treasury's reporting of estimated jobs created or retained as a result of the interim SSBCI loans may duplicate data reported by the SBA loan program.

Further, Idaho mistakenly overstated by $111,923 the total principal for 3 of 42 loans we reviewed because the amounts reported were not based on the final loan documents. The inaccurate amount for one of the three loans was included in the State's *2012 Annual Report* and must be corrected. Alerted by our audit, Idaho corrected the other two before they were published in the State's *2013 Annual Report*. The State also inaccurately reported $781,000 as Treasury-approved subsequent private financing, which Treasury acknowledged was due to inconsistent guidance to the State. Finally, although Treasury reduced Idaho's allocation for unsupported administrative costs charged to the program between January 2012 and September 2012, we determined that administrative costs charged since then were reasonable, allowable, and allocable in accordance with the *SSBCI Policy Guidelines* and OMB Circular A-87.

We recommend that Treasury disclose in its next annual report the borrower's number of jobs created and retained that were associated with bridge loans to businesses that may receive permanent financing through the SBA CDC/504 loan program, and remind states that reported loan amounts must be based on final loan agreements. We also recommend that Treasury instruct Idaho to correct the amount of loan originations and subsequent private financing reported in its *2012 Annual Report*, determine whether the State has defaulted on its

---

[9] Rounded up from $9,562,897.
[10] Rounded down from $1,306,574.

Allocation Agreement for inaccurately reporting loan amounts, and if so, take appropriate action.

Treasury disagreed with recommendation 1, but proposed to explain clearly in its *Summary of States' Annual Reports* that there is a possibility for duplicate reporting of job creation and retention figures, which was responsive to the audit finding. Treasury also accepted recommendations 2, 3 and 4, stating it would work with Idaho to resolve the erroneous reporting of subsequent private financing and incorrect loan originations, and to determine whether the inaccurate reporting of loan amounts constitutes a general event of default. Formal written responses from Treasury and from Idaho are included in their entirety in Appendix 2.

Background

SSBCI is a $1.5 billion Treasury program that provides participating states, territories, and eligible municipalities with funds for Capital Access Programs and other credit support programs that provide financial assistance to small businesses and manufacturers. Other credit support programs include collateral support, loan participation, loan guarantee, and venture capital programs.

Collateral support programs provide additional collateral for small businesses and manufacturers that are creditworthy, but are not getting the loans they need. The collateral is held by the lender until the loan is repaid, and then returned to the state. Each participating state or territory is required to designate specific departments, agencies, or political subdivisions to implement the programs approved for funding. The designated state entity distributes SSBCI funds to various public and private institutions, which may include a subdivision of another state, a for-profit entity supervised by the state, or a non-profit entity supervised by the state.

These entities use funds to make loans or provide credit access to small businesses. Primary oversight of the use of SSBCI funds is the responsibility of each participating state. To ensure that funds are properly controlled and expended, the Act requires that Treasury execute an *Allocation Agreement* with participants setting forth internal controls and compliance and reporting requirements before allocating SSBCI funds.

Treasury disburses SSBCI funds to participants in three payments: the first when the Secretary approves the state for participation, and the second and third after the participant certifies that it has obligated, transferred, or spent at least 80 percent of the previous allocation. In addition, the participant is required to certify that it has complied with all applicable program requirements.

Idaho's Participation in SSBCI

In August 2011, Treasury approved Idaho's SSBCI application and awarded the State approximately $13.2 million. The Governor of Idaho designated the Idaho Department of Commerce to receive SSBCI funds and to implement and oversee the State program. The Idaho Department of Commerce has contracted with IHFA (a non-profit entity supervised by the State) for the administration of ICSP. IHFA is authorized to use allocated SSBCI funds only for the purposes and activities specified in the State's *Allocation Agreement* with Treasury, including for direct and indirect administrative costs.

The State's SSBCI *Allocation Agreement* directed the entirety of Idaho's allocation to support ICSP. ICSP is a collaborative partnership between the Treasury, Idaho Department of Commerce, IHFA, and the Idaho Bankers Association. ICSP establishes pledged cash collateral accounts with participating lenders to enhance loan collateral for qualified small business borrowers who would not otherwise be able to obtain financing on acceptable terms and conditions. The collateral deposits are established on an individual loan basis and are available to cover loan losses in the event of default by the borrower.

By December 31, 2011, Treasury had disbursed the first payment of the State's allocation, $4.3 million.[11] Treasury reviewed the administrative expenses that Idaho claimed from January 2012 to

---

[11] Rounded down from $4,345,556.

September 2012 and found that $31,806 in expenses were not adequately supported in accordance with OMB Circular A-87. Consequently, on May 10, 2013, Treasury reduced Idaho's allocation to approximately $13.1 million. As of September 30, 2013, Idaho had received all of its revised allocation amount and had obligated or expended $12.7 million, representing 96 percent of the State's total SSBCI award, on collateral deposits for 124 loans with an aggregate loan value of approximately $78.2 million.[12] The State also used $272,744 for administrative costs associated with ICSP. Like all of SSBCI's other credit support programs, ICSP must demonstrate a 1:1 private leveraging ratio, meaning that the SSBCI funds will spur additional lending, using non-federal funds, that is equal to or greater than the amount of lending supported by SSBCI funds.

Idaho Used Funds Appropriately, But Financed Loans that May Cause Duplicate Reporting of Benefits from SBA CDC/504 Loan Program

We determined that the State of Idaho properly used the SSBCI funds we tested. All of the 42 transactions reviewed complied with program guidelines related to use of proceeds, capital-at-risk, maximum transaction amounts, and other restrictions noted in the Act and *SSBCI Policy Guidelines*. Idaho also collected complete borrower and lender assurances.

However, we identified 5 loans, totaling approximately $9.8 million[13] and supported by $1.3 million[14] in SSBCI collateral, that provided interim financing of real estate acquisitions, construction projects, or equipment purchases that had been approved for the Small Business Administration's (SBA) Certified Development Company (CDC)/504 loan program. SBA's CDC/504 loan program provides small businesses with long-term fixed-rate financing to acquire major fixed assets, such as equipment or real estate. Under the CDC/504 program, a CDC provides the borrower two loans – one secured from

---

[12] Rounded up from $78,189,061.
[13] Rounded down from $9,806,619.
[14] Rounded down from $1,306,574.

a private lender and one from the CDC that is backed by a 100-percent SBA-guaranteed debenture.

Interim financing is typically needed to bridge the period between SBA approval of the project and replacement of the interim financing with a permanent debenture. Idaho officials explained that once the debenture is issued, the long-term financing is put in place and the interim lender releases the SSBCI-funded collateral support back to the State.

During the interim period, the lender provides 90 percent of the borrower's needed financing, a higher credit exposure than under traditional commercial credit guidelines. The SBA will issue its permanent debenture only if there is no "unremedied substantial adverse change" in the borrower's condition. The SBA 504/CDC loan program does not cover construction or renovation period, so the borrower must complete this work during the interim period, which may continue over a year in some cases. During the interim period, the lender bears the full credit risk of the borrower, as well as the risk that the borrower incurs cost overruns or construction delays. If there is an "unremedied substantial adverse change" in the borrower's condition during the interim period, the SBA may not issue the permanent debenture and the interim loan will not be repaid. This is the rationale for Idaho's CSP to offer credit support to lenders for the bridge loans.

SSBCI Policy Guidelines explicitly prohibit the enrollment of SBA-guaranteed loans in states' SSBCI programs. However, Treasury officials stated that an SSBCI-supported bridge loan is permitted because the SBA-supported loan would repay the loan supported by SSBCI collateral. Therefore, SBA does not support the transaction at the same time as the SSBCI-supported loan.

We noted, however, that the SBA CDC/504 loan program and SSBCI have similar goals of helping small businesses and manufacturers create and maintain jobs, and both programs report these job statistics as program accomplishments. All SSBCI participants are required to report annually the borrower's estimate of jobs created/retained with

SSBCI funding. Treasury reports these estimates annually as a summary of states' annual reports. With respect to the CDC/504 program, businesses assisted must create or retain one job for every $65,000 provided by the SBA, and small manufacturers must create or retain one job for every $100,000 guaranteed by the SBA. Therefore, Treasury's reporting of jobs created or retained by recipients of SSBCI supported loans may potentially duplicate the accomplishments reported by the SBA.

The CDC/504 program guarantees long-term loans, while the SSBCI funding is used for short-term loans that bridges the period between SBA approval of the project and replacement of the interim financing with a debenture. Therefore, Treasury should disclose in its next annual report entitled, *State Small Business Credit Initiative: A summary of States' 2013 Annual Reports*, the amount of jobs created and retained that were associated with bridge loans to businesses that received SBA guarantees.

Idaho Did Not Accurately Report Amount of Loans Supported by SSBCI Funds

Of the 42 loans tested, Idaho inaccurately reported the loan amounts (called loan originations) for 3 loans enrolled in ICSP as of September 30, 2013. The inaccurate amount for one of the loans was included in Idaho's *2012 Annual Report*. Alerted by our audit, Idaho corrected the other two loan amounts in the State's *2013 Annual Report*.

The inaccurate reporting resulted in a net overstatement of loan originations by $111,923. The overstatement occurred because IHFA reported the loan amounts listed on the lenders' applications for ICSP, instead of reporting the loan principal shown on final loan agreements provided by the lenders. Prior to loan closing, lenders changed the principal amounts for the three loans from that listed on the applications, but did not inform IHFA of the changes. Accurate reporting of total loan originations is important because Treasury uses this information to determine whether a state meets the private leverage ratio requirement. If total loan originations are inaccurate, then the private leverage ratio will be inaccurate as well.

According to the *Allocation Agreement* signed by Idaho, inaccurate reporting can trigger a general event of default of the agreement. Treasury will need to determine whether such an event has occurred, and if so, whether it warrants a reduction, suspension or termination of future funding to the State. Furthermore, to ensure the accuracy of the information, Treasury should remind states to report loan amounts based on final loan agreements, rather than loan applications. Treasury will also need to instruct Idaho to correct the amount of loan orginations it reported for 2012.

Idaho Reported Subsequent Private Financing Without Explicit Approval from Treasury

In its *2012 Annual Report,* Idaho reported $781,000 in subsequent private financing resulting from SSBCI collateral support without explicit approval from Treasury. Subsequent private financing is additional lending that a borrower obtains from a private source as a direct result of the increased creditworthiness that the borrower gained from the assistance received from SSBCI. The information is used by Treasury to compute the State's private leverage ratio achieved with SSBCI funds.

The SSBCI *Allocation Agreement* signed by Idaho states that collateral support programs do not directly add assets to a company's balance sheet that improve its creditworthiness for further loans or investments. Therefore, the State was not eligible to report subsequent private financing resulting from its collateral support program unless Treasury reviewed the program and gave the State explicit permission to do so.

Idaho sought and received approval from Treasury to report $500,000 in subsequent private financing for one transaction, but reported an additional $781,000 from two other transactions without explicit approval from Treasury. The State was not to blame because Treasury officials informed us that they had given Idaho inconsistent guidance on the issue. Alerted by our audit, the State corrected the figure in its *2013 Annual Report*, but the State's *2012 Annual Report* included the unapproved subsequent private financing. Treasury will need to instruct Idaho to remove the amount of subsequent private financing for the two transactions from the 2012 report.

Idaho's Administrative Expenses Were Allowable, Allocable, and Reasonable

Treasury reviewed the administrative expenses that Idaho claimed from January 2012 to September 2012, leading Treasury to reduce Idaho's final allotment by $31,806 for expenses that were not adequately supported in accordance with OMB Circular A-87. As of September 30, 2013, Idaho had spent an additional $272,744 in administrative expenses, or 2 percent of the SSBCI funds transferred to the State. Our review of 100 percent of the $272,744 in administrative expenses that Idaho incurred between September 2012 and September 2013 found they were allowable, allocable, and reasonable in accordance with *SSBCI Policy Guidelines* and Office of Management and Budget (OMB) Circular A-87, *Cost Principles for State, Local, and Indian Tribal Governments*.

Recommendations

We recommend that the Deputy Assistant Secretary for Small Business, Housing, and Community Development:

1. Disclose in its next annual SSBCI report, titled *State Small Business Credit Initiative: A Summary of States' 2013 Annual Reports,* the number of jobs reported as created or retained by SSBCI programs that may be duplicated by reports of jobs created or retained by the SBA CDC/504 program.

2. Remind states to report loan amounts based on final loan agreements, rather than loan applications.

3. Instruct Idaho to correct the amount of loan originations and delete the subsequent private financing for the two transactions identified by the audit from its *2012 Annual Report*.

4. Determine whether the inaccurate reporting of loan amounts constitutes a general event of default, and if so, whether funding to Idaho should be reduced, suspended, or terminated.

Management Comments and OIG Response

We provided a draft of the report to Treasury on April 24, 2014, and received formal written responses from Treasury and from Idaho on May 14, 2014. Treasury disagreed with recommendation 1 in theory and in practice, stating that jobs could not be allocated separately to the SSBCI and SBA CDC/504 programs. Treasury also stated that as a practical matter, neither Treasury nor the states receive information that would allow it to determine whether a small business loan backed by SSBCI funding was repaid with an SBA CDC/504 loan. However, Treasury proposed alternatively to explain clearly in the *Summary of States' Annual Reports* that there is a possibility for duplicate reporting of job creation and retention figures. We consider Treasury's proposed action to be responsive to recommendation 1. Treasury accepted recommendations 2, 3, and 4, stating that it would work with Idaho to resolve the erroneous inclusion of subsequent private financing and incorrect loan originations in Idaho's 2012 report, and determine whether the inaccurate reporting of loan amounts constitutes a general event of default. Responses from Treasury and from the state of Idaho are included in their entirety in Appendix 2.

* * * * * *

We appreciate the courtesies and cooperation provided to our staff during the evaluation. If you wish to discuss the report, you may contact me at (202) 622-1090, or Clayton Boyce, Audit Director, at (202) 927-5642.

/ s /

Debra Ritt
Special Deputy Inspector General for
Office of Small Business Lending Fund Program Oversight

Appendix 1: Objective, Scope, and Methodology

The objective of our audit was to test Idaho's compliance with the Small Business Jobs Act of 2010 (the Act) and State Small Business Credit Initiative (SSBCI) program requirements and prohibitions to identify reckless or intentional misuse of funds. As of September 30, 2013, Idaho had received all of its revised allocation of approximately $13.1 million[15] and had obligated or spent approximately $12.7 million[16] of the funds through the Idaho Collateral Support Program (ICSP).

The scope of our audit included small business loans enrolled in ICSP from August 12, 2011, the date of Idaho's approval as an SSBCI participant, to September 30, 2013. During this period, the Idaho Housing and Finance Association (IHFA) enrolled or supported 124 loans in ICSP with a total loan value of $78.2 million[17] and committed or reserved collateral support funds for 12 loans with a proposed principal value of approximately $10.8 million.[18] In addition, as of September 30, 2013, Idaho had recycled into ICSP approximately $1.3 million[19] from collateral support funds returned to IHFA after the SSBCI-supported loans were paid in full.

To test participant compliance, we reviewed a sample of 30 loans made by 14 lending institutions that were enrolled in ICSP as of September 30, 2013. We also reviewed 12 loans that were to be enrolled in ICSP and for which SSBCI funds had been committed or reserved as of September 30, 2013. We performed testing to ensure such loans complied with the requirements and prohibitions of the Act, *SSBCI Policy Guidelines, SSBCI National Standards for Compliance and Oversight, Frequently Asked Questions,* and other Treasury guidance. We judgmentally selected the sampled loans based on the materiality of the loan, while ensuring that diverse lenders were selected. We reviewed the electronic loan files provided by IHFA staff and compared the information in the loan files to specific requirements and prohibitions of the Act and Treasury guidelines.

---

[15] Rounded down from $13,136,544.
[16] Rounded up from $12,655,537.
[17] Rounded up from $78,189,061.
[18] Rounded down from $10,814,704.
[19] Rounded down from $1,322,423.

We sent written inquiries to IHFA staff responsible for administering, managing, accounting for, and reporting on ICSP on behalf of the Idaho Department of Commerce. We also reviewed associated policies, procedures, and other written guidance provided by IHAF related to the use of SSBCI funds. We conducted our audit between December 2013 and March 2014 in accordance with *Government Auditing Standards*. Those standards require that we plan and perform the audit to obtain sufficient, appropriate evidence to provide a reasonable basis for our findings and conclusions based on our audit objectives. We believe that the evidence obtained to address our audit objectives provides a reasonable basis for our findings and conclusions.

Appendix 2: Management Response

DEPARTMENT OF THE TREASURY
WASHINGTON, D.C. 20220

May 14, 2014

Ms. Debra Ritt
Special Deputy Inspector General for
  Office of Small Business Lending Fund Program Oversight
U.S. Department of the Treasury
1500 Pennsylvania Avenue, NW
Washington, DC 20220

Dear Ms. Ritt:

Thank you for the opportunity to review the Office of the Inspector General's (OIG) draft report entitled *State Small Business Credit Initiative: Idaho's Use of Funds for its Collateral Support Program* (the Report). This letter provides the official response of the Department of the Treasury (Treasury).

We appreciate the Report's finding that Idaho used State Small Business Credit Initiative (SSBCI) funds appropriately and that all of the reviewed transactions complied with SSBCI program requirements. However, the report also identified two instances of reporting irregularities and asks Treasury to determine whether the inaccurate reporting constitutes a general event of default. With your consent, Treasury transmitted a copy of the Report to Idaho program officials on April 25, 2014. Treasury asked Idaho to provide a narrative response describing the measures it has taken or plans to take to address the deficiencies noted in the Report.

In its reply, enclosed, Idaho states that the State appreciates the Report's recommendations and offers responses to the audits findings. Idaho asserts that the State has corrected the erroneous reporting of loan originations in its 2013 annual report and implemented new controls to ensure that the amount reported is the actual amount of the executed loan. Idaho also comments that they will work with Treasury to rectify the erroneous inclusion of subsequent private financing and incorrect loan origination amounts in their 2012 report. Treasury accepts recommendations two, three, and four of the Report and will work with Idaho to resolve them accordingly, including determining whether the inaccurate reporting of loan amounts constitutes a general event of default.

The Report's first recommendation raises legal and operational hurdles that will prevent Treasury from implementing the recommendation exactly as written. The Report asks Treasury, in its next annual report, to disclose the number of jobs reported as created or retained by SSBCI programs that may duplicate the reported jobs created or retained by the SBA CDC/504 program.

Ms. Dejma Ring
May 14, 2014
Page 2 of 2

Treasury disagrees with this recommendation in theory and in practice. Many states require each program to report the estimated number of jobs created or retained. Because both the SSBCI Program and SBA CDC/504 program provided credit support at different times during the construction project, jobs cannot be allocated separately to the two programs. Moreover, as a practical matter, neither Treasury nor the states receive information that would allow it to determine whether a small business loan backed by SSBCI funding was repaid with a permanent loan from the SBA CDC/504 program.

In response to the Report's first recommendation, Treasury agrees to explain clearly in the summary of States' Annual Reports that there is a possibility of double counting of jobs created and retained figures. Unfortunately, Treasury is unable to report the exact number of jobs that are also reported by other programs.

Thank you once again for the opportunity to review the Report. Treasury appreciates our work together throughout the course of the SSBCI program.

Sincerely,

Amias M. Gerety
Acting Assistant Secretary
Office of Financial Institutions

Enclosure

C.L. "Butch" Otter, Governor
Jeffery Sayer, Director

April 29, 2014

Mr. Don Graves, Jr.
Deputy Assistant Secretary
Small Business, Community Development and Affordable Housing Policy
U.S. Department of Treasury
Washington, D.C. 20220

RE: State Small Business Credit Initiative: Idaho's Use of Funds for its Collateral Support Program

Dear Mr. Graves:

Idaho Housing and Finance Association (IHFA) has received the Audit Report from the Office of Inspector General (OIG) and appreciate the recommendations and the opportunity to respond.

As it pertains to the specific findings of the Audit Report, we submit the following responses:

Finding #2
Idaho Did Not Accurately Report Amount of Loans Supported by SSBCI Funds

Idaho CSP Account Number	Loan Principal per Bank Documents	Loan Amount Reported in Program Activity	Difference
6786000230008	$1,422,095.40	$1,440,095.00	$ 17,999.60
3435000210012	$ 600,000.00	$ 700,000.00	$100,000.00
2325373500007	$1,206,077.00	$1,200,000.00	($ 6,077.00)
			$111,922.60 Net

The required annual reporting to Treasury SSBCI for FYE 12/31/2013 included the correct enrolled lender loan originations for the two loans enrolled in Idaho CSP in 2013 in the amounts of $1,422,095.40 and $600,000. This reporting was due on or before March 30, 2014. As the ongoing OIG audit brought this discrepancy to light prior to completing the 2013 report, the correct loan origination (based off the Bank's loan documentation) amounts were reported by IHFA in the 2013 annual report. No further correction should be necessary regarding the FYE 2013 report.

Therefore, the only outstanding issue that requires action is to increase the reported loan origination (Idaho CSP account #2325373500007) by $6,077.00 in the FYE 12/31/2012 annual report on this enrolled lender loan.

Controls were implemented beginning in February of 2014 which now require a copy of the Bank's promissory note to verify the actual/final loan origination amount prior to funding the collateral support deposit account on the enrolled lender loan. With the implementation of this new control, the required annual reporting is based off the Bank's loan origination document as opposed to the loan amount disclosed on the Idaho CSP Application.

Finding #3
Idaho Reported Subsequent Private Financing Without Explicit Approval from Treasury

A conference call was held with Treasury SSBCI on January 27, 2014. From that conversation, it was the consensus that the subsequent private financing reported on Idaho's FYE 12/31/2012 report would be excluded from the report. In order to correct this transaction in the FYE 12/31/2012 report, Treasury SSBCI needs to "open" the report to allow IHFA to make this correction. Once IHFA is advised by Treasury that the FYE 2012 report can be accessed, the correction will be made to exclude the subsequent private financing from Idaho's FYE 12/31/2012 SSBCI report.

IHFA appreciates the professional manner in which the OIG Audit Team performed this audit. Thank you for the opportunity to provide a response to the recommendations identified in the Audit Report.

Regards,

Jeff Sayer
Director
Idaho Department of Commerce

Appendix 3: Major Contributors

Debra Ritt, Special Deputy Inspector General

Clayton Boyce, Audit Director

Sara Emiline Tete Nkongo, Auditor-in-Charge

Ai Jun A. Wang, Auditor

Karin Beam, Referencer

Appendix 4: Distribution List

Department of the Treasury

Deputy Secretary
Office of Strategic Planning and Performance Management
Risk and Control Group

Office of Management and Budget

OIG Budget Examiner

United States Senate

Chairman and Ranking Member
Committee on Small Business and Entrepreneurship

Chairman and Ranking Member
Committee on Finance

Chairman and Ranking Member
Committee on Banking, Housing, and Urban Affairs

Chairman and Ranking Member
Committee on Homeland Security and Governmental Affairs

Chairman and Ranking Member
Appropriations Subcommittee on Financial Services and General Government

United States House of Representatives

Chairman and Ranking Member
Committee on Small Business

Chairman and Ranking Member
Committee on Financial Services

Chairman and Ranking Member
Committee on Oversight and Government Reform

Chairman and Ranking Member
Appropriations Subcommittee on Financial Services and General Government

Government Accountability Office

Comptroller General of the United States

www.ingramcontent.com/pod-product-compliance
Lightning Source LLC
Chambersburg PA
CBHW081824170526
45167CB00008B/3535